LEVEL ONE ▼ MIXED

ESSENTIAL REPERTOIRE

FOR THE YOUNG CHOIR

BY
JANICE KILLIAN
MICHAEL O'HERN
LINDA RANN
EDITED BY
EMILY CROCKER

ISBN 0-7935-4223-5

HAL•LEONARD™
CORPORATION
7777 W. BLUEMOUND RD. P.O. BOX 13819 MILWAUKEE, WI 53213

AUTHORS

Dr. Janice Killian, Music Education
Texas Woman's University, Denton, Texas

Michael O'Hern, Choral Director
Lake Highlands Junior High
Richardson Independent School District, Texas

Linda Rann, Choral Director
Dan F. Long Middle School
Carrollton-Farmers Branch Independent School
District, Texas

PROJECT EDITOR
Emily Crocker
Director of Choral Publications
Hal Leonard Corporation, Milwaukee, Wisconsin

PRODUCTION EDITOR
Ryan French
Choral Editor
Hal Leonard Corporation, Milwaukee, Wisconsin

CONSULTANTS
Glenda Casey, Choral Director
Berkner High School
Richardson Independent School District, Texas

Bobbie Douglass, Choral Director
L. D. Bell High School
Hurst-Euless-Bedford Independent School District,
Texas

Jan Juneau, Choral Director
Klein High School
Klein Independent School District, Texas

Dr. John Leavitt, Composer and Conductor
Wichita, Kansas

Brad White, Choral Director
Richland High School
Birdville Independent School District, Texas

Send all inquiries to:
Hal Leonard Corporation
7777 W. Bluemound Rd., Box 13819
Milwaukee, WI 53213

CONTENTS

 # TO THE STUDENT

Welcome to choir!

The reason students join choir are as diverse as the students themselves. Whatever your reason may be, this book was designed to help you achieve your particular goal. The many different types of songs in this book have been selected to fit your voice and allow you to be successful. In music, just as in many other activities, practice, effort, and dedication will pay off. Your study of choral music can develop skills that you will enjoy throughout your entire life. Best wishes for your musical success!

Student Expectations Checklist:

- Take responsibility for your own development as a musician.
- Every time you sing, make it a quality experience.
- Work to master the basic musical skills.
- Develop an attitude of wanting to improve every day.
- Be willing to try new things.
- Display an attitude of effort at all times.
- Come to class prepared to work and learn.
- Be present for all rehearsals and performances.
- Listen carefully during rehearsals. Critical listening improves the quality of a choir.
- Show a willingness to work with others.
- Choir is a "group" effort, but every individual counts. Working together is the key.
- Respect the effort of others.
- Practice concert etiquette at all times, especially during rehearsals.
- Make a positive contribution, don't be a distraction to the choir.
- Enjoy experiencing and making beautiful music.

CANTATE DOMINO (SING TO THE LORD, OUR GOD)

Composer: Giuseppi Ottavio Pitoni (1657-1743), edited by John Reed
Text: Latin Psalm Text, English Translation by James Pruett
Voicing: SATB a cappella

Cultural Context:

Giuseppi Pitoni (1657-1743) was an eminent church musician who lived in Italy during the *Baroque Period*. Sacred choral music was very important at this time and many church composers continued to write in the polyphonic choral style that was popular a century earlier in the *Renaissance*. Pitoni used all Latin texts in his sacred works like "Cantante Domino." His music often incorporated *polyphony* (each voice is equally important and enters at a different time) with occasional *homophony* (music in which the parts move together with the same rhythm).

During this period, musical notation was still developing; as a result, metrical barlines, dynamics, and other style markings were not included in the music. The markings you see in this edition were all added by the editor, John Reed. Sometimes, the meter shifts for a brief time. Notice how the triple meter changes in measures 25-30.

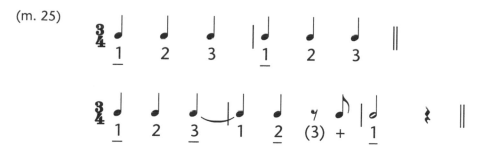

(m. 25)

Where else does this meter shift occur? This shifting is called *hemiola*.

Musical Terms:

allegro	*mf* (mezzo forte)	⌢p (fermata)
f (forte)	*mp* (mezzo piano)	polyphony
homophony	hemiola	*cresc.* (crescendo)
——— (decrescendo)	*p* (piano)	

Preparation:
Practice saying the Latin words in the phonetic pronunciation guide below.

Cantate Domino, canticum novum:
KAHN-tah-teh DAW-mee-naw KAHN-tee-koom NAW-voom

Laus ejus in Ecclesia Sanctorum,
LAH(oo)s EH-yoos een eh-KLEH-zee-ah SAHNK-taw-řoom

Laetetur Israel in eo,
leh-TEH-tooř EEZ-řah-ehl een EH-aw

Qui fecit eum: et filiae Sion, exultent in rege suo.
quee FEH-cheet EH-oom eht FEE-lee-eh SEE-awn ehk-ZOOL-tehnt een ŘEH-jeh SOO-aw

*ř = flipped or rolled r.

Practice your good choral skills by repeating the following words with good, tall, open vowel sounds.

Evaluation:
Speak the text in rhythm in the following ways and evaluate your Latin pronunciation and rhythmic precision.

- All together
- In sections

Cantate Domino

(Sing To The Lord, Our God)

For SATB a cappella

By GIUSEPPI OTTAVIO PITONI (1657-1743)
Edited and Arranged by JOHN REED

English translation by JAMES PRUETT

ta - te, can - ta - te Do - mi - no, can - ti - cum
sing we to God, Now praise we our Mak - er, now

ta - te, can - ta - te Do - mi - no, can - ti - cum
sing we to God, Now praise we our Mak - er, now

ta - te, can - ta - te Do - mi - no, can - ti - cum
sing we to God, Now praise we our Mak - er, now

ta - te, can - ta - te Do - mi - no, can - ti - cum
sing we to God, Now praise we our Mak - er, now

no - vum: Laus e - jus in Ec - cle - si - a
praise we our Mak - er, Now ex - tol Him, ye

no - vum: Laus e - jus in Ec - cle - si - a
praise we our Mak - er, Now ex - tol Him, ye

no - vum: Laus e - jus in Ec - cle - si - a
praise we our Mak - er, Now ex - tol Him, ye

no - vum: Laus e - jus in Ec - cle - si - a
praise we our Mak - er, Now ex - tol Him, ye

San - cto - rum, in Ec - cle - si - a San -
saints, O ye hosts, O ye hosts of saints, ye

San - cto - rum, in Ec - cle - si - a San -
saints, O hosts, O ye hosts of saints, ye

San - cto - rum, in Ec - cle - si - a San -
saints, O hosts, O ye hosts of saints, ye

San - cto - rum, in Ec - cle - si - a San -
saints, O hosts, O ye hosts of saints, ye

cto - rum. Lae - te - tur Is - ra - el
hosts of saints. Come now and all re - joice

cto - rum. Lae - te - tur Is - ra - el
hosts of saints. Come now and all re - joice

cto - rum. Lae - te - tur Is - ra - el
hosts of saints. Come now and all re - joice

cto - rum. Lae - te - tur Is - ra - el
hosts of saints. Come now and all re - joice

5

DIDN'T MY LORD DELIVER DANIEL

Composer: Spiritual adapted and arranged by Roger Emerson
Text: Traditional
Voicing: 3-Part Mixed

Cultural Context:

Spirituals developed in America before the Civil War when slaves turned to Biblical stories to create music of hope and relief from oppression and suffering. In this spiritual, if the Lord could deliver Daniel from a den of lions and Jonah from the belly of a whale, why could the Lord not deliver the slaves from bondage?

Musical Terms:

(♩ = 80)   (♩ = 132-144)   *mp* (mezzo piano)

mf (mezzo forte)   *cresc.* (crescendo)   *f* (forte)

unis. (unison)   div. (divisi)   ₚ̄ (tenuto)

rit. (ritardando)   ₚ̆ (accent)   ⨁ Coda

D.S. al Coda   𝄋 (sign)   **To Coda**

⌢ₚ (fermata)   syncopation

Preparation:

Syncopation is a rhythmic pattern that stresses notes on the "offbeat." Practice these syncopated patterns:

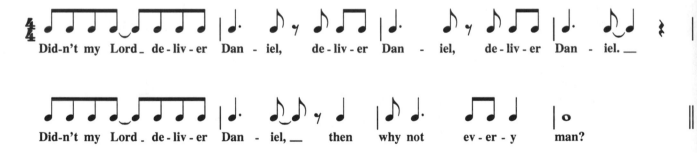

Notice how much rhythmic energy syncopation adds. Syncopated rhythm is a characteristic of African-American spirituals and now is used in many other styles of music.

Evaluation:

• Record the choir singing this song. When you listen, quietly tap or conduct the steady beat. Do you hear and feel the syncopation in this song?

• What other spirituals of deliverance or hope have you sung or heard? Share your experiences in small or large group discussion.

Didn't My Lord Deliver Daniel

For 3-Part Mixed Voices and Piano

Traditional Spiritual
Adapted and Arranged by ROGER EMERSON

whale, and the He-brew chil - dren from the fier-y fur-nace, then

Fm7 Eb/G Ab F7 Bbm7 Fm7 Eb/G Ab Fm7

cresc.
div.
why not ev-er-y man?
cresc.

Unis. *f*
Did-n't my Lord __ de-liv-er

Csus C Fm9
cresc.
f

Dan - iel, __ de-liv-er Dan - iel, __ de-liv-er Dan - iel. __

Bbm7 Fm9

14

DING DONG! MERRILY ON HIGH!

Composer: Traditional carols, arranged by Ed Lojeski
Text: Traditional
Voicing: SATB a cappella

Cultural Context:
This arrangement is a lively setting of the 16th century French carol "Ding Dong! Merrily on High!," combined with the 16th century English carol "Good King Wenceslas." In addition, the arranger has added a *madrigal*-like contrasting section which introduces and then accompanies "Good King Wenceslas."

Musical Terms:

f (forte)   *p* (piano)   *pp* (pianissimo)

ff (fortissimo)   *cresc.* (crescendo)   ⌢ (fermata)

Preparation:
Practice singing the passage below:

1. Practice it once using the syllable "too." Be sure to stress the first beat of every measure.
2. Practice singing it again on the text, using the following dynamics:
   - 1st time – forte
   - 2nd time – pianissimo

Practice saying the words written below using the word stress indicated.

HIGH - est   SING - ing   GLO - ry   RING - ing

Evaluation:
Record your choir singing "Ding Dong! Merrily on High!" Listen for the following:

1. Word Stress – Are you stressing the first syllable more than the second of the words listed above?
2. Dynamic change – Are you singing the dynamics marked in the score?
3. Rhythmic precision – On the long "Gloria" phrases, can you hear the separate notes clearly?

Ding Dong! Merrily On High!

For SATB a cappella

Performance Notes: Keep tempo bright throughout. This arrangement can be performed by any size group with a minimum of rehearsal time.

Old French Carol
Arranged by ED LOJESKI (ASCAP)

ri - a! Sing glo - ry to the

ri - a! Sing glo - ry to the

Glo - ri - a! Sing glo - ry to the

Glo - ri - a! Sing glo - ry to the

High - est.

High - est.

High - est.

High - est. Glo

Fa la la la la la la.   Fa la la fa la la

Fa la la la.   Fa la la la la la la.

22

Fa la la la la la la. Fa la la fa la la

Fa la la la. Fa la la

la. Fa la la la la la la.

la. Fa la la la.

mf

Fa la la la.

24

25

Fa la la fa la la la.

Fa la la la.

Fa la la la la la. Bright - ly shone the

deep and crisp and e - ven. Bright - ly shone the

moon that night tho the frost was cru - el.

moon that night. tho the frost was cru - el.

27

29

—ri - a! Sing glo - ry to the High - est!

—ri - a! Sing glo - ry to the High - est!

a! Sing glo - ry to the High - est!

a! Sing glo - ry to the High - est!

82

pp

Glo - ri -

pp

Glo

pp

Glo

82

pp

30

ECCE QUAM BONUM (SEE HOW GOOD, HOW RIGHT)

Composer: Jean Richafort (1480-1548), edited by Maynard Klein
Text: Latin text adapted from Psalm 133
Voicing: SATB a cappella

Cultural Context:

Jean Richafort (ca. 1480-1548) lived during a time period known as the *Renaissance* (1450-1600). The Renaissance is sometimes called the "Golden Age of A Cappella Music" because of the large number of unaccompanied choral pieces written during that time.

"Ecce Quam Bonum," like other Renaissance choral music, is *polyphonic*. Polyphonic means that each voice is equally important and enters at a different time throughout the piece. Notice the polyphonic entrances in "Ecce Quam Bonum."

Many characteristics of our modern musical notation were developed after this music was written. The meter, barlines, and style words (dynamics, tempo markings, articulations) were all added by the editor, and are only suggestions for how the music should be performed.

Musical Terms:

a cappella	polyphonic	Renaissance
melisma	allegro	(♩ = c. 120)
mf (mezzo forte)	*mp* (mezzo piano)	animato
f (forte)	*ff* (fortissimo)	legato
staccato	——————— (crescendo and decrescendo)	

Preparation:

Melismas (patterns which contain more than one note per word syllable) may be a challenge in this piece. Use the following exercise to practice singing melismas cleanly. Do not let notes run together.

1. Sing the notes staccato (short) on a neutral syllable.
2. Sing the notes legato (connected).
3. Separate the notes just slightly (a combination of legato and staccato).

Evaluation:

Look at your music and circle the melismas in your part. Your circles should remind you to sing these patterns cleanly without running the notes together. As you rehearse "Ecce Quam Bonum," check to see if you are performing the melismas cleanly.

Ecce Quam Bonum

(See How Good, How Right)

For SATB a cappella

Psalm 133
Adapted by M. K.

Music by JEAN RICHAFORT (c. 1480-1548)
Edited by MAYNARD KLEIN

34

GLORIA FESTIVA

Composer: Emily Crocker
Text: Traditional Latin with additional words by Emily Crocker
Voicing: 3-Part Mixed

Cultural Context:

"Gloria Festiva" was written in 1993 by Emily Crocker, a Texas native who now lives and composes in Milwaukee, Wisconsin. She has published music since 1980, and has over 100 choral pieces in print. A portion of the text in "Gloria Festiva" is traditional Latin.

Musical Terms:

(♩ = ca. 132)   *mp* (mezzo piano)   *mf* (mezzo forte)

ff (fortissimo)   *decresc.* (decrescendo)   ⌢ (fermata)

cresc. (crescendo)   *dolce*   *al fine*

maestoso   *rit.* (ritardando)   opt. div. (optional divisi)

descant   *f* (forte)   (no breath)

Preparation:

Pronunciation: *Gloria in excelsis Deo,*
                   GLAW-řee-ah een ehk-SHEHL-sees DEH-aw

                   et in terra pax hominibus.
                   eht een TEH-řah pahks aw-MEE-nee-boos

                   *ř = flipped or rolled r.

Translation: Glory to God in the highest, and peace on earth to all.

• Tap, clap, or count the rhythm pattern below. Be sure to observe the rest on the second half of beat 3 in the first measure of the phrase.

• Chant the Latin words to this rhythm.

Evaluation:

To perform this song successfully, sing pure Latin vowels with rhythmic accuracy. As you sing the first 22 measures, answer the following questions:

1. Did I sing with tall, pure Latin vowels?

2. Did my vowel sounds blend with the other singers around me?

3. Did I sing the words in precise rhythm?

4. Was I rhythmically precise with the other singers around me?

5. Did I sing with energy?

As you master the song, continue to evaluate your progress.

Gloria Festiva

For 3-Part Mixed Voices and Piano

Traditional Latin
With additional Words and Music by
EMILY CROCKER (ASCAP)

With jubilance (♩ = ca. 132)

Glo - ri - a _____ in ex - cel - sis De - o,

et in ter - ra pax ho - mi - ni - bus.

Glo - ri - a _____ in ex - cel - sis De - o,

et in ter - ra pax ho - mi - ni -

13 Unis.

𝆑

Glo - ri - a _____ in ex - cel - sis De - o,

bus.

et in ter - ra pax ho - mi - ni - bus

Glo - ri - a _____ in ex - cel - sis De - o,

Glo - ri - a _____ in ex - cel - sis De - o,

et in ter - ra pax ho - mi - ni - bus.

et in ter - ra pax ho - mi - ni - bus.

join the might-y throng._____ Glo-ri - a _____ in ex-

join the might-y throng. Glo-ri - a _____ in ex-

cel - sis De - o, et in ter - ra

cel - sis De - o, et in ter - ra

pax ho - mi - ni - bus. Glo-ri - a _____ in ex-

pax ho - mi - ni - bus. Glo-ri - a _____ in ex-

cel - sis De - o,   et in ter - ra

cel - sis De - o,   et in ter - ra

pax ho - mi - ni - bus.

pax ho - mi - ni - bus.

41 *dolce*
mp

Come all re - joice   in the light _____

Re - joice in the

mp dolce

42

and ban - ish fear and

light.

sor - row. O won - d'rous

and ban - ish sor - row.

love, sur - round us,

O won - d'rous love.

44

45

46

GOOD TIMBER GROWS

Composer: Roger Emerson
Text: Anonymous
Voicing: SATB a cappella

Cultural Context:
Roger Emerson said this about the music he wrote:
"The text is paramount in this selection. Therefore, do not rush, enunciate very clearly, and allow time and space for the textual ideal to become firmly implanted in the listener's mind."

Musical Terms:

(♩ = ca. 69) adagio rubato

p (piano) ⌢𝆒 (fermata) *mp* (mezzo piano)

rit. (ritardando) // (caesura) *decresc.* (decrescendo)

sub. (subito) *a tempo* *f* (forte)

cresc. poco a poco (crescendo poco a poco)

Preparation:
Say the words in the text printed below as marked with stressed and unstressed syllables, crescendo and decrescendo. Place your two hands in front of you. Physically move them apart on the crescendo and back together on the decrescendo as if playing an accordian or stretching a rubber band.

p

Good TIM-ber_____DOES not GROW in ease.

mp

Good TIM-ber_____DOES not GROW in ease.

cresc. poco a poco

The STRONG-er WIND, _____the STRONG-er TREES; _____

sub. mp

The FAR-ther sky, _____the GREAT-er length _____

increased intensity

The more the STORMS, the MORE the STRE _____ngth;

mp

By SUN or COLD, _____by RAIN and SNOW, _____

_____ *slowly* _____ *(fade out)*

In TREE or MAN, _____Good TIM-ber GROWS.

Evaluation:
Study the poem (text) carefully. Write a short essay on what the poem means to you. What is the connection between "good people" and "good timber"? Can you find other poetry that compares humankind to nature? Do you enjoy singing this song? Why or why not?

Good Timber Grows

For SATB a cappella

ANONYMOUS

Music by ROGER EMERSON

49

50

JU ME LEVE UN BEL MAITÍN (IN THE MORNING I AROSE)

Composer: Anonymous, edited by Robert L. Goodale
Text: Anonymous, 15th Century
Voicing: SATB a cappella

Cultural Context:

As you read the translation of the text, you will discover that it tells a story. Perhaps the character in the poem lived in the northeast corner of Spain near the French border – thus the use of the three languages: Spanish, French, and Catalan. (Catalan is spoken in the northeast corner of Spain.)

A song of this type is called a *villancico*, a short 16th century song with several stanzas linked by a refrain. The villancico composer often worked with the poet to tell the story with a new style of musical expression.

"Din-di-rin-daña" are nonsense syllables, such as "la-la-la" used today.

The markings (dynamics, tempo, style words) were all added by the editor, Robert L. Goodale.

Musical Terms:

ritard. (ritardando) f (forte)   *poco ritard.* (poco ritardando)

mf (mezzo forte) $\frown$ (fermata) p (piano)

vivace e leggiero pp (pianissimo)   ¢ (cut time)

————————— (crescendo)

Preparation:

Sing the following rhythms on a neutral syllables. Be sure to stress beat 1 more than beats 2 and 3. Practice forte the first time and piano the second time. This exercise should have a light, dance-like quality.

Evaluation:

Record your choir singing this piece and listen for the following:

    • Are you stressing beat 1 more than beats 2 and 3?

    • Are you singing the dynamics indicated by the editor?

Ju Me Leve un Bel Maitín
(In the Morning I Arose)

For SATB a cappella

15th Century Villancico
Translated and Edited by ROBERT L. GOODALE

53

A JUBILANT PSALM

Composer: Emily Crocker
Text: Adapted from Psalms 8 and 67
Voicing: SATB

Cultural Context:

This exciting, high-energy piece was written by Emily Crocker in 1991 for a special concert by the Brandenburg Middle School Choir in Garland, Texas.

"A Jubilant Psalm" is written in contrasting styles. The first part is energetic, fast, and accented. Label it "A." The second section (beginning in measure 19) is marked dolce (sweetly) and is to be sung in a soft, sustained manner. Label it "B." Are there any sections of this piece which repeat? Which set of letters best describes the structure of "A Jubilant Psalm" — "AB" or "ABA"?

Musical Terms:

con spirito	(♩ = 138)	(♩ = 152)
f (forte)	*mf* (mezzo forte)	*mp* (mezzo piano)
div. (divisi)	cresc. (crescendo)	(decrescendo)
dolce	*poco a poco*	*piu forte*
syncopated	*molto rit.* (molto ritardando)	Tempo I

Preparation:

Practice the following patterns for rhythmic precision in "A Jubilant Psalm."
1. Steady eighth notes:

2. Syncopated eighth notes:

3. Words + syncopated eighth notes:

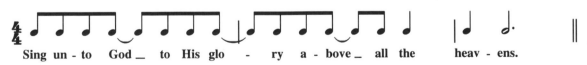

Sing un - to God _ to His glo - ry a - bove _ all the heav - ens.

Evaluation:

Can your choir speak the phrase, "Sing unto God, to His glory above all the heavens," precisely together? To check precision, stand in a circle so you can hear each other clearly. Speak the phrase again, emphasizing each beginning consonant. Is each word precisely together and can each word be understood? Repeat this exercise with the sung phrase and with other phrases from the piece.

To the Brandenburg Middle School A Cappella Choir, Garland, Texas;
for their 1991 National A.C.D.A. Concert, Debbie Helm, Director

A Jubilant Psalm

For SATB and Piano

Adapted from Psalms 8 and 67

Music by EMILY CROCKER (ASCAP)

lu - ia, al -le - lu - ia!

lu - ia, al -le - lu - ia!

lu - ia, al -le - lu - ia!

al -le -lu - ia, al -le - lu - ia!

All na - tions be glad and

Now all be glad and

Now all be glad and

Now all be glad and

59

sing _____ for joy. Pro - claim His glo - ry in

sing for joy. _____ Pro - claim His glo - ry in

sing for joy. Pro - claim His glo - ry in

sing for joy. Pro - claim His glo - ry in

mf *cresc. poco a poco*

ev - 'ry land. Oh God, be

mf *cresc. poco a poco*

ev - 'ry land. Oh God, be

mf cresc. poco a poco

ev - 'ry land. Oh God, be

mf cresc. poco a poco

ev - 'ry land. Oh God, be

marcato cresc. poco a poco

gra - cious and bless us _____ and make your

gra - cious and bless us _____ and make your

gra - cious and bless us _____ and make your

gra - cious and bless us _____ and make your

sim.

face to shine up - on us, _____ that your

face to shine up - on us. _____

face to shine up - on us, _____ that your

face to shine up - on us. _____

61

way   may be   known   on the   earth _____

Sing un - to God ___ in the   high - est! _____

way   may be   known   on the   earth _____

Sing un - to God ___ in the

___   and your   pow'r   a - mong   all

___   Sing un - to God ___ in the   high - est!

___   and your   pow'r   a - mong   all

high - est! _____

na - tions.

Sing un - to God__ in the high - est!

na - tions.

Sing un - to God__ in the high - est!

44 *piu forte*

div.

Sing un - to God__ to His glo - ry a - bove__ all the heav - ens!

piu forte

Sing un - to God__ to His glo - ry a - bove__ all the heav - ens!

piu forte

Sing un - to God__ to His glo - ry a - bove__ all the heav - ens!

piu forte

Sing un - to God__ to His glo - ry a - bove__ all the heav - ens!

44

piu forte

R.H.

Sing to His name_ all ye peo - ple who dwell_ on the earth! Al - le-

Sing to His name_ all ye peo - ple who dwell_ on the earth! Al - le-

Sing to His name_ all ye peo - ple who dwell_ on the earth! Al - le-

Sing to His name_ all ye peo - ple who dwell_ on the earth!

lu - ia, al - le - lu - ia, al - le - lu - ia! Al - le - lu - ia!

lu - ia, al - le - lu - ia, al - le - lu - ia! Al - le - lu - ia!

lu - ia, al - le - lu - ia, al - le - lu - ia! Al - le - lu - ia!

Al - le - lu - ia, al - le - lu - ia, al - le - lu - ia! Al - le - lu - ia!

* Sing lower notes only if the upper Tenor notes are out of range.

65

66

JUBILATE! JUBILATE!

Composer: Russian Air, arranged by Joyce Eilers
Text: Samuel Longfellow
Voicing: 3-Part Mixed a cappella

Cultural Context:

Samuel Longfellow, brother of noted poet, Henry Wadsworth Longfellow, wrote the text used in "Jubilate! Jubilate!" He was born in Portland, Maine, in June 1819 and died there in 1892. Longfellow received his BA degree from Harvard (1839) and the BD (Bachelor of Divinity) degree from the Harvard Divinity School (1846). This hymn was first included in Longfellow's book *Vespers* (1859), a collection of hymns for the Second Unitarian Church. The hymn tune honors the end of another day and the wonder of creation.

Musical Terms:

(♩ = 112-120)   *mp* (mezzo piano)   *mf* (mezzo forte)

pp (pianissimo)   :‖ (repeat sign)   *f* (forte)

◁▷ (crescendo and decrescendo)

Preparation:

This piece utilizes 4-bar phrases throughout. Practice this breathing exercise using only one breath. (Repeat as often as needed to perform in one breath.) When you are ready, add the words as found in your music.

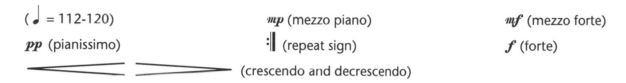

The following phrases present a real challenge for Part III, because they are so similar. Can you sing them?

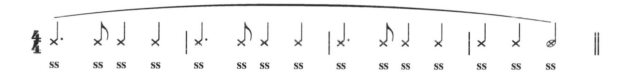

Evaluation:

Record the choir singing this work a cappella (no accompaniment). As you listen to the tape, listen for the following:

1. Can you hear the 4-bar pharses? Listen to make sure that no one is breathing after only 2 bars of music.
2. Is Part III singing the correct pitches in measures: 3, 7, 13, 17, 33, 37, 43, 47, 53, 57?
3. Continue practicing the preparation exercises until you can successfully sing this song with 4-bar phrases and correct pitches.

Jubilate! Jubilate!

For 3-Part Mixed Voices a cappella

Performance Notes: This piece uses careful voice leading, limited ranges, optimum use of dynamics, and retains the dignity without difficulty that is the essence of this masterwork.

Words by SAMUEL LONGFELLOW (1819-1892)

RUSSIAN AIR
Arranged by JOYCE EILERS

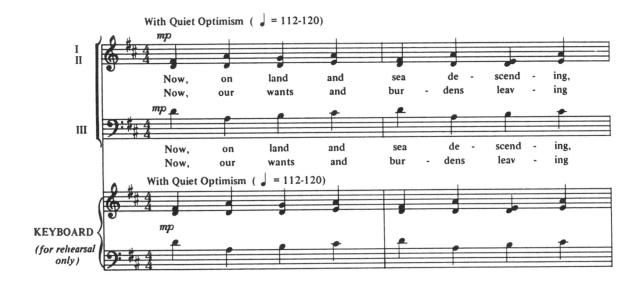

Now, on land and sea de - scend - ing,
Now, our wants and bur - dens leav - ing

brings the night its peace pro - found. Let our ves - per
to His care who cares for all. Cease we fear - ing,

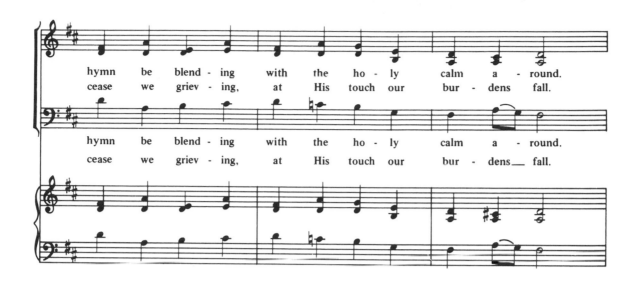

hymn be blend - ing with the ho - ly calm a - round.
cease we griev - ing, at His touch our bur - dens fall.

hymn be blend - ing with the ho - ly calm a - round.
cease we griev - ing, at His touch our bur - dens___ fall.

9 Joyful

*Ju - bi - la - te! Ju - bi - la - te! Ju - bi - la - te!

*Ju - bi - la - te!___ Ju - bi - la - te! Ju - bi - la - te!___

9

13

A - men! Let our ves - per hymn be blend - ing
Cease we fear - ing, cease we griev - ing,

A - men! Let our ves - per hymn be blend - ing
Cease we fear - ing, cease we griev - ing,

13

* Pronounced "you - bih - lah - teh"

69

with the ho - ly___ calm a - round. Let our ves - per
At His touch our___ bur - dens fall. Cease we fear - ing,

hymn be blend - ing with the ho - ly___ calm a - round.
cease we griev - ing, at His touch our___ bur - dens fall.

As the dark - ness deep - ens o'er us, Lo! E - ter - nal stars a - rise.

shin - ing in the ___ spir - it's skies. Hope and faith and

shin - ing in the spir - it's ___ skies. Hope and faith and

love rise glo - rious, shin - ing in the ___ spir - it's skies.

love rise glo - rious, shin - ing in the spir - it's ___ skies.

Soon as dies the sun - set glo - ry, stars of heav'n shine

Soon as dies the sun - set glo - ry, stars of heav'n shine

72

out a - bove. tell - ing still the an - cient sto - ry,

out a - bove. tell - ing still the an - cient sto - ry,

their Cre - a - tor's change - less love. Ju - bi - la - te!

their Cre - a - tor's change - less love. Ju - bi - la - te!

Ju - bi - la - te! Ju - bi - la - te! A - men!

Ju - bi - la - te! Ju - bi - la - te! A - men!

THE MIRACLE OF HANUKKAH

Composer: Emily Crocker
Text: Emily Crocker
Voicing: 3-Part Mixed

Cultural Context:

Hanukkah is a Jewish observance commemorating the rededication of the Temple of Jerusalem (165 B.C.). Judas Maccabeus led a small band of Jews to successfully overthrow the Syrians (Greeks) and retake the Jewish Temple. The celebration also recalls the legend of how a small, one-day supply of oil miraculously burned in the Temple for eight full days until new oil could be obtained. Thus, Hanukkah is known as the Feast of Lights. Each night of the eight-day celebration a candle is lit on a special candlestick called a menorah. It is a joyous family celebration of prayers, games, gifts, and meals.

Musical Terms:

(♩ = 100)   *mf* (mezzo forte)   *cresc.* (crescendo)

f (forte)   *ff* (fortissimo)   ᷤ (accent)

♩ (cued notes)

Preparation:

• Look at measure 23 as printed below. Notice that the melody line, the rhythm patterns, and the words are different for each part.
• Practice singing each melody separately in unison.
• Now sing the three melodies together as written.

Measure 23

Evaluation:

As you rehearse and perform this selection, can you hear the three separate melodies? Are they equally balanced or is one part too loud? Learn to listen carefully to the other sections of your choir.

The Miracle Of Hanukkah

For 3-Part Mixed Voices and Piano

Words and Music by EMILY CROCKER

77

81

MUSIC, MOST WONDROUS, LOVELY ART (MUSICA, DIE GANZ LIEBLICH KUNST)

Composer: Johann Jeep (ca. 1581-1644), edited by John Leavitt
Text: Anonymous, German by Johann Jeep, English translation by John Leavitt
Voicing: SATB a cappella

Cultural Context:

"Music, Most Wondrous, Lovely Art" was written almost 400 years ago during the *Renassiance Period*. Jeep used a style of composing called *polyphony* in which each voice part begins at a different place, is independent and important, and sections of the music often repeat in a contrasting dynamic level. "Music, Most Wondrous, Lovely Art" is written for *a cappella voices* (without instrumental accompaniment). The words pay tribute to the art of music and the music is written in a light and flowing texture.

Musical Terms:

andante   (♩ = ca. 68)   *mf* (mezzo forte)

p (piano)   *f* (forte)   𝄐 (fermata)

𝄆 𝄇 (repeat signs)

Preparation:

- A good example of polyphony is mm. 12-16 printed below. Notice how each part has a different rhythm pattern causing the words to fall on different beats in the measure.
- As each section becomes secure in both rhythm and pitch, begin to sing the parts together.

Evaluation:

Brainstorm in small groups and list the popular songs of today which you think will still be sung by choral groups and schools in the year 2400. Make a list of at least five songs. Compare your list with other lists in the class. What qualities must a song possess to last for 400 years? Is it the words, the melody, the organization of the notes on a page, or the challenge of learning it? Why do you feel this song has lasted?

Music, Most Wondrous, Lovely Art

(Musica, die ganz lieblich Kunst)

For SATB a cappella

By JOHANN JEEP (ca. 1581-1644)
Edited by JOHN LEAVITT

PRAISE THE LORD WITH JOYFUL SONG

Composer: Early American Hymn Tune, arranged by Hal H. Hopson
Text: Based on the Psalm 95 (Venite Exultemus)
Voicing: 3-Part Mixed

Cultural Context:

Hal Hopson, a resident of Dallas, Texas, arranges much sacred music for young voices. This arrangement is based on the early American Hymn tune "Boundless Mercy."

Musical Terms:

rit. (ritardando)　　　　　(♩ = ca. 116)　　　　　*f* (forte)

ff (fortissimo)　　　　　*mf* (mezzo forte)　　　　　*p* (piano)

a tempo

Preparation:

1. Three separate melodies are found in this song. Can you identify where each melody begins?

   • Practice each melody in unison.

   • Now sing the three melodies together as they are shown in mm. 65-72. Keep the eighth note patterns very clean and steady.

2. The shape of each line is one of the most important musical elements in "Praise the Lord with Joyful Song." Practice the following exercise paying particular attention to the phrase markings indicated.

Evaluation:

• As you rehearse and perform this selection, can you hear the three separate melodies?

• Are they equally balanced, or is one part too loud?

• Learn to listen carefully to the other sections of your choir.

Praise The Lord With Joyful Song

For 3-Part Mixed Voices and Piano

Paraphrased from Psalm 95

Early American Tune
"Boundless Mercy"
Arranged by HAL H. HOPSON

Spirited, but not too fast (♩ = ca. 116)

Organ or Piano

1. Praise the Lord with joy - ful_ song; hail the Rock who saves us.

Of - fer God our grate - ful_ hearts, shout our loud thanks -

forth their praise;__ hills re-flect His good -ness. The o-ceans al - so

forth their praise; hills re-flect His good - ness. O - ceans al - so

tell__ of__ God;__ the dry land He cre - at - ed. God__ made__ all the

tell of__ God; dry land He cre - at - ed. God made all the

earth and__ sky,__ all__ cre - a - tion's splen - dor.

earth and__ sky, all cre - a - tion's splen - dor.

94

PSALLITE

Composer: Attributed to Michael Praetorius, edited by Henry Leck
Text: English text by Henry Leck
Voicing: SATB a cappella

Cultural Context:

Michael Praetorius (1571-1621) is one of the most famous composers of the early *Baroque Period*. He is also remembered for his work in music theory and compiling hymns.

"Psallite" is written in two languages, Latin and German. During this time the entire church service was performed in Latin, and most of the sacred music composed was also written in Latin. When Praetorius wrote "Psallite," he was working at a church in Germany. He wrote in Latin and German to please both the clergy and the members of the German congregation.

The style markings and dynamics were all added by the editor, Henry Leck, and did not appear in the original notation.

Musical Terms:

Allegro

f (forte)

$\overset{>}{\mathbb{P}}$ (accent)

p (piano)

mp (mezzo piano)

pp (pianissimo)

◁───── (crescendo)

mf (mezzo forte)

─────▷ (decrescendo)

Preparation:

Practice saying the Latin and German words in the phonetic pronunciation guide below.

Latin:
Psallite, unigenito, Christo Dei Filio.
SAH-lee-teh OON-nee-JEH-nee-taw KR̃EE-staw DEH-ee FEE-lee-aw

Redemptori Domino puerulo
R̃EH-dehm-TAW-r̃ee DAW-mee-naw poo-EH-r̃oo-law

jacenti in praesepio.
yah-CHEN-tsee EEN pr̃eh-SEH-pee-aw

German:
Ein Kleines Kindelein liegt in dem Krippelein.
Ah(ee)n KLAH(EE)N-es KIHN-deh-lah(ee)n leekt EEN deh(ee)m KR̃IHP-uh-lah(ee)n

Alle liebe Engelein dienen dem Kindelein,
AH-leh LEE-beh EHNG-uh-lah(ee)n DEE-nehn deh(ee)m KIHN-deh-lah(ee)n

Und singen ihm fein.
Oont ZING-ehn eem fah(ee)n

* r̃ = flipped or rolled r.

Evaluation:

Speak the text in rhythm in the following ways, and evaluate both pronunciation and rhythmic precision.

1. All together
2. In sections

Psallite

For SATB a cappella

English Text by HENRY LECK

By MICHAEL PRAETORIUS (1571-1621)
Edited by HENRY LECK

in prae - se - pi - o.
Je - sus Christ our Lord.

Ein klei - nes Kin - de - lein liegt in dem Krip - pe -
A lit - tle child so sweet lies in a lit - tle

in prae - se - pi - o.
Je - sus Christ our Lord.

Ein klei - nes Kin - de - lein liegt in dem Krip - pe -
A lit - tle child so sweet lies in a lit - tle

in prae - se - pi - o.
Je - sus Christ our Lord.

in prae - se - pi - o.
Je - sus Christ our Lord.

lein.
crib.

lein.
crib.

Al - le lie - be En - ge - lein die - nen dem
Love - ly an - gels serve the child and sing to the

Al - le lie - be En - ge - lein die - nen dem
Love - ly an - gels serve the child and sing to the

SEASON'S GREETINGS

Composer: Traditional Holiday Songs, arranged by Joyce Eilers
Text: Traditional Secular Carols
Voicing: SATB

Cultural Context:

This medley can be used as a holiday concert finale and/or audience sing-along. The songs in the medley include: "Deck the Hall," "Up on the Housetop," "Jolly Old St. Nicholas," "Over the River and Through the Woods," and "Jingle Bells."

All of these secular carols should have a light, festive feel. The tone should never get heavy.

Musical Terms:

‖: :‖ (repeat signs)　　　　　*sub.* (subito)　　　　　*div.* (divisi)

sim. (simile)　　　　　⌐1.⌐ (first ending)　　　　　⌐2.⌐ (second ending)

// (caesura)　　　　　*f* (forte)　　　　　*mf* (mezzo forte)

◁———▷ *cresc.* (crescendo)　　　*mp* (mezzo piano)　　　♩ ♩ (no breath)

Preparation:

"Over the River and Through the Woods" is written in 6/8 time. Chant both verses in rhythm.

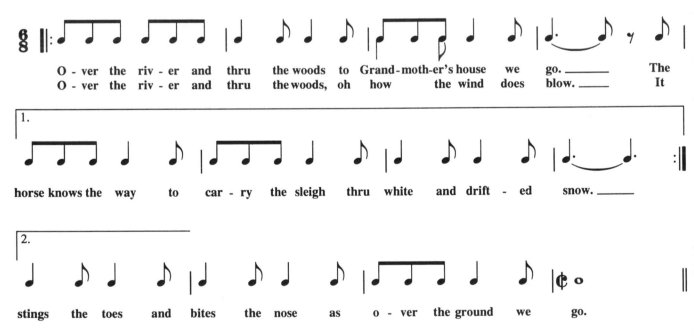

Evaluation:

Create choreography for this medley that reflects a light, festive feel. The movements, like the tone, should never get heavy.

Season's Greetings

(A Holiday Concert Finale)

Deck The Halls • Jingle Bells • Jolly Old St. Nicholas
Over The River And Through The Woods • Up On The Housetop

For SATB and Piano with Optional Instrumental Accompaniment

Performance Note: This is a winter concert finale/celebation of five secular holiday songs
Enjoy!

Instrumental Arrangement by
PAUL JENNINGS

Arranged by
JOYCE EILERS

Good Saint Nick! Who? Good Saint, Jol - ly old Saint Nich - o - las,

lean your ear this way! Don't you tell a

sin - gle soul what I have to say!

Christ-mas Eve is com-ing soon; now you dear old man,

tell me what you'll bring for me. Tell me if you

can.

108

68 Sleigh Bells

o - ver the ground we go.

72 JINGLE BELLS

Jin - gle bells,

jin - gle bells, jin - gle all the way.

110

SEND DOWN THE RAIN

Composer: Joyce Eilers
Text: Joyce Eilers
Voicing: 3-Part Mixed

Cultural Context:
Joyce Eilers was raised on a farm in Oklahoma. This song, dedicated to her parents, compares the restless desert farmland to our own human emotions. She writes that the idea for this song came to her while on a visit to England. However, the lush green English countryside was not the right environment to create the song that she heard in her mind, and it was not until she returned to the dry Oklahoma prairie that the song could be written.

As you learn the song, notice how the music reflects the meaning of the lyrics.

Musical Terms:

syncopation

mf (mezzo forte)

pp (pianissimo)

(decrescendo)

rit. (ritardando)

f (forte)

p (piano)

(fermata)

cresc. (crescendo)

mp (mezzo piano)

, (breath mark)

Preparation:
Syncopation is a rhythmic pattern that stresses notes on the "off beat." Practice the following syncopated rhythms.

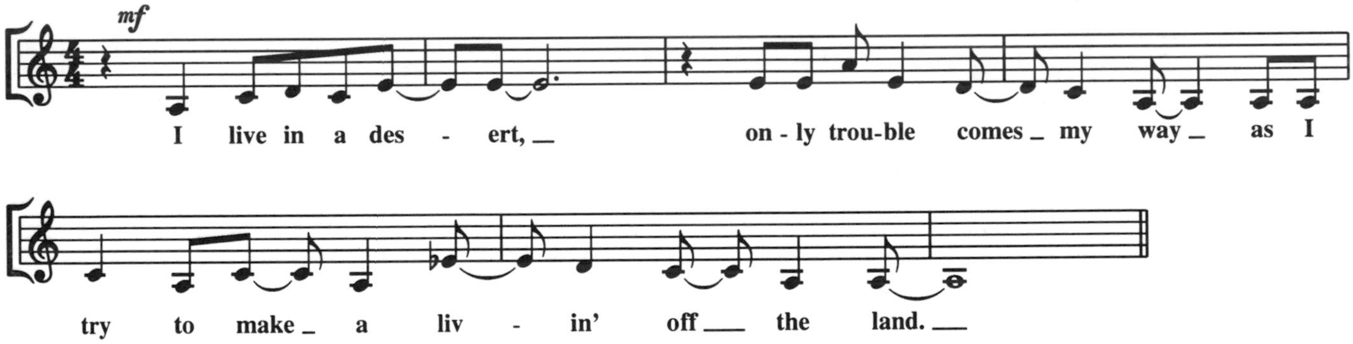
mf
I live in a des - ert, _ on - ly trou-ble comes _ my way _ as I
try to make _ a liv - in' off ___ the land. ___

Evaluation:
Can you identify other syncopated sections in this piece? Practice these sections for rhythmic precision.

For my parents, Mr. and Mrs. Fred Eilers, Mooreland, Oklahoma

Send Down The Rain

For 3-Part Mixed Voices and Piano

Words and Music by JOYCE EILERS

Part I and II or Unison

I live in a des- ert,___ on-ly trou-ble comes___ my way___ as I

try to make_ a liv- in' off__ the land.___

114

115

116

Send down the rain. _____ Oh, Lord, I

Send down the rain. _____ Send down the rain, _____

Send down the rain. _____ Oh, Lord, I

see the light- nin', ____ Oh, Lord, I hear the thun- der. ___ hooo

_____ Send down the rain, _____ Send down the rain. hooo

see the light- nin', ____ Oh, Lord, I hear the thun- der. ___ hooo

SHENANDOAH

Composer: American Folk Song, arranged by Linda Spevacek
Text: Traditional
Voicing: SATB

Cultural Context:

This familiar American folk song refers to the sorrow early American settlers felt as they left their homes and moved westward to cross the wide Missouri River. Originally "Shenandoah" was a sea chantey sung by sailors longing for home. In some versions of this song, Shenandoah refers to a river (the Shenandoah River in Virginia); in others it refers to a region of the country (Shenandoah River valley); and in still others it refers to the people of the region ("Oh Shenandoah, I love your daughter"). Regardless of the precise meaning of the word, this beautiful song still describes the sadness and loneliness all people, from whatever time, have felt as they prepare to leave familiar places.

Musical Terms:

(♩ = 76-80)   *ten.* (tenuto)   *cresc.* (crescendo)

rit. (ritardando)   *a tempo*   *mp* (mezzo piano)

p (piano)   *mf* (mezzo forte)   (♩ = 92-52)

————————— (decrescendo)   Tempo I   *molto rit.* (molto ritardando)

Preparation:

Try this exercise to prepare for the long phrases and pure vowels this piece demands.
1. Breathe deeply and sing a pitch on "oo."

  • Count slowly to 8, 12, or 16 as you sing. Breathe deeply.

  • Try to sing "away you rollin' river" on one breath.

2. A *diphthong* is two vowels sung together. Remember to hold the first vowel and put the last vowel on the very end. It is so short that it is almost unheard.

  • Sing the word "way" and hold it for 8, 12, or 16 beats. Notice that when you sing "ay" you are really singing "eh-ee."

  • Sing the word "wide" and hold it for 8, 12 or 16 beats. "I" in "wide" is also a diphthong and is really pronounced "ah-ee."

  • Try singing the diphthong in "bound" as "ah-oo."

Did you sing the diphthong correctly? Try to sing diphthongs correctly as you rehearse "Shenandoah."

Evaluation:

After you have learned the rhythms and pitches of this song, sing the first two pages and ask yourself these questions as you are singing.

1. Can I sing each phrase on one breath?

2. Can I sing each diphthong in these phrases correctly? Each diphthong is underlined.

   O Shenando' I long to see you, a<u>way</u> you rollin' river.

   O Shenando' I long to see you, a<u>way</u>, we're b<u>ou</u>nd a<u>way</u>, 'cross the <u>wide</u> Missouri.

120

Shenandoah

For SATB and Piano

American Folk Song
Arranged by LINDA STEEN SPEVACEK

121

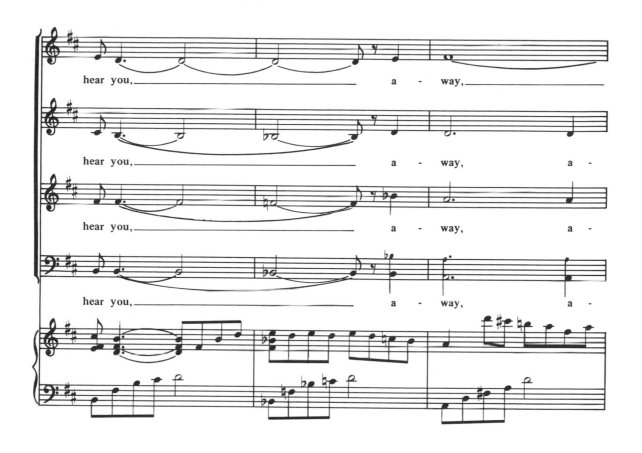

hear you,_____ a - way,_____

hear you,_____ a - way, a -

hear you,_____ a - way, a -

hear you,_____ a - way, a -

rit.

_____ we're bound a - way,_____ 'cross the

- way, we're bound a - way, 'cross the

- way, we're bound a - way, 'cross the

- way, we're bound a - way, 'cross the

127

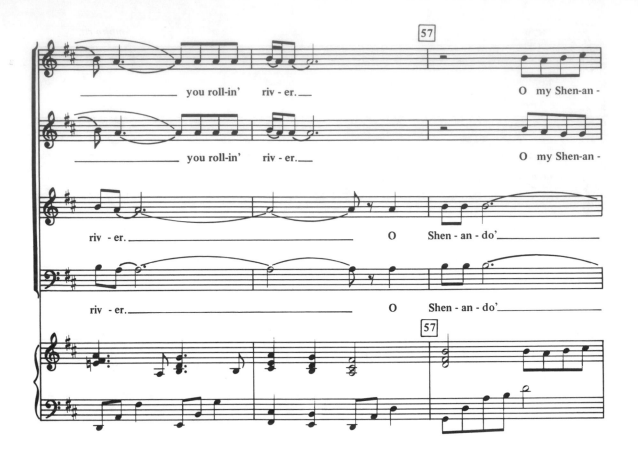

128

129

130

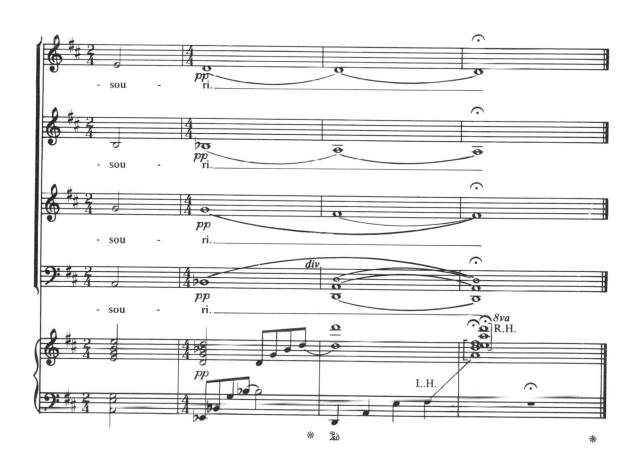

SING PRAISE, ALLELUIA

Composer: Emily Crocker
Text: Emily Crocker
Voicing: 3-Part Mixed

Cultural Context:

"Sing Praise, Alleluia" was written in 1983 by Emily Crocker. This festival piece displays contrast between the rhythmic, energetic opening and ending, and the smooth, *legato* middle section.

Musical Terms:

f (forte)   *p* (piano)   cresc. (crescendo)

mp (mezzo piano)   *molto ritard.* (molto ritardando)   *a tempo*

⌢ (fermata)   > (accent)   (dotted barline)

Preparation:

Rhythmic accuracy is important for a successful performance of this piece. The eighth note is constant throughout. You will notice a dotted barline in several places in this piece. The dotted barline indicates the notes to be stressed in the bar, in this case, the first and fourth eighth notes. Find the dotted barlines in "Sing Praise, Alleluia."

In order to learn to keep a steady rhythm, practice this rhythm pattern in two groups:

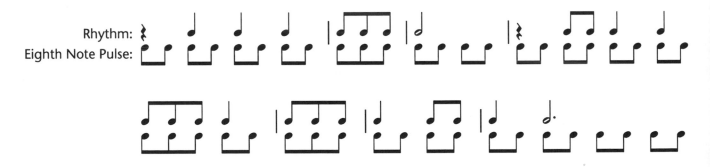

Evaluation:

To check for accuracy of the ryhthm in the first nine measures of this song, have one half of the class tap a steady eighth note pulse (you may want to use a metronome) while the other half chants the opening text in rhythm.

Are you skilled enough to keep the eighth note constant throughout?

Sing Praise, Alleluia

For 3-Part Mixed Voices and Piano

Words and Music by EMILY CROCKER

133

137

Crea - tures of the earth praise His name! Sing praise un-

Crea - tures of the earth praise His name! Sing praise un-

Crea - tures of the earth praise His name! Sing praise un-

to ____ the Lord. Let us make a joy - ful noise

to ____ the Lord. Let us make a joy - ful noise

to ____ the Lord. Let us make a joy - ful noise

un - to the Lord. Al - le - lu - ia! _____ Al - le-

un - to the Lord. Al - le-

un - to the Lord. Al - le-

lu - ia! A - men. _____

lu - ia! A - men. _____

lu - ia! A - men. _____

139

SINNER MAN

Composer: Traditional Spiritual, arranged by Roger Emerson
Text: Traditional
Voicing: 3-Part Mixed

Cultural Context:

"Sinner Man" is an arrangement of a well-known spiritual. It is so well-known that you may already know some version of this song. Spirituals were developed by African American slaves and have become an influential part of American culture. You can probably name many spirituals. You might start with "Swing Low, Sweet Chariot." How many others do you know?

Musical Terms:

Freely (♩ = 69-72)   spiritual   ⌢ (fermata)

Driving rock (♩ = 120-138)   ♩ (accent)   ‾ (tenuto)
                            >

♩ (staccato)   hushed   **p** (piano)

mf (mezzo forte)   ***f*** (forte)   *cresc.* (crescendo)

syncopated   ♩‑‑‑♩ (no breath)

Preparation:

This arrangement of "Sinner Man" is interesting because it asks the choir to change moods for each verse. Each section is quite different. Look at your music and find how each section is changed. Can you answer just by looking at the music, or do you need to hear it first?

   Introduction (*Oh sinner man,* mm. 1-8)

   Verse 1 (*Run to the rock,* mm. 12-19)

   Verse 2 (*Run to the sea,* mm. 20-28)

   Verse 3 (*Oh sinner man, should a been a prayin',* mm. 28-37)

   Verse 4 (*Oh sinner man, where you gonna run to,* mm. 38-end)

Evaluation:

After you have learned the pitches and rhythms of this song, make a copy of the following graph showing how each verse of "Sinner Man" should be performed. Write one word in each square.

	Slow/Fast	Loud/Soft	Syncopated/Not Syncopated
Intro			
Verse 1			
Verse 2			
Verse 3			
Verse 4			

Now sing the song. Are you performing each verse exactly as indicated in the music?

Sinner Man

For 3-Part Mixed Voices and Piano with Optional Rhythm Section

Spiritual
Adapted and Arranged by ROGER EMERSON

141

142

143

144

THE TURTLE DOVE

Composer: Traditional English Folk Song, arranged by Linda Spevacek
Text: Traditional
Voicing: 3-Part Mixed with Flute (optional)

Cultural Context:

This beautiful folk song describes the sorrow of leaving a loved one. That pain is compared with the sound of a turtle dove mournfully cooing in the distance. The song is a promise to return ("though I roam ten thousand miles") and a promise to remain faithful ("till the stars fall from the sky"). Like most folk songs, "The Turtle Dove" has been handed down from generation to generation.

Read the words to yourself and enjoy singing the beautiful melody that goes with them.

Musical Terms:

unison	*a tempo*	*rit.* (ritardando)
molto rit. (molto ritardando)	*mp* (mezzo piano)	*f* (forte)
(fermata)	*p* (pianissimo)	// (caesura)
(tenuto)		

Preparation:

A. Having enough breath to sing through each phrase may be a challenge in this piece. To prepare, try this exercise. You may have to repeat it several times.

- Breathe deeply and read each line slowly on one breath.

  Fare you well my dear I must be gone and leave you for awhile.

  If I roam away I'll come back again tho' I roam ten thousand miles my dear.

B. Correct diction of words which contain diphthongs may be a problem in this piece. A diphthong is two vowels sung together to make one continuous sound.

1. Sing and hold "i" words (while, mile, right) on a pitch .

- Notice that when you sing the "i" of "while" you are really singing "AH-(ee)."

- When singing in English, the last vowel in a diphthong is put at the very end. It is so short that it is almost not heard.

2. Circle each word in "The Turtle Dove" that has an "i" sound. The circles will remind you to sing the diphthong correctly.

Evaluation:

After you have learned the rhythms and pitches of this song, pay special attention to how you personally are singing "i" diphthongs. Are you singing them correctly? Are you holding the "ahhhh"? Is there too much "ee"? As you sing other songs, pay attention to how accurately you are singing "i" diphthongs.

The Turtle Dove

For 3-Part Mixed Voices and Piano with Optional Flute

Traditional English Folk Song
Arranged by LINDA SPEVACEK

**May use humming, second keyboard or another appropriate instrument if flute is not used or omit all together.
*Harp may be substituted for keyboard.

while. If I roam a - way I'll come back a - gain, tho' I

cresc.

roam ten thou - sand miles, my dear, tho' I roam ten thou - sand

rit. *rit.* *f* *rit.*

17 *a tempo*

a tempo

miles. _____

17 *a tempo* *mf* *p* *sim.*

150

lit - tle tur - tle dove, he doth

O___ yon - der sits that lit - tle tur - tle dove, he doth

sit on___ yon - der high tree, a____

sit on yon - der tree,_____

making a moan, for the loss of his love as

as

I will do for thee, my dear, as I will do for

I will do for thee, my dear, as I will do for

molto rit.

molto rit.

molto rit.

molto rit. L.H.

The Turtle Dove

FLUTE

Traditional English Folk Song
Arranged by LINDA SPEVACEK

WE BELONG

Composer: Linda Spevacek
Text: Linda Spevacek
Voicing: SATB

Cultural Context:
The words to this song have an extremely important message. Read them to yourself before you begin learning the song.

Verse
Some people you and I may know are born with a diff'rent skin.
They live in many diff'rent ways in places we've not been.
But it matters not in this great big world, whether they are black, yellow, red or white,
No it matters not in this great big world, together in spirit we are all as one.

Chorus
Oh, we belong and you belong together in one family,
Let the world now celebrate and live in perfect harmony.
We belong and you belong together in one family.
Here we stand, united we stand, strong in spirit we are all as one.

Verse
If ev'ryone would take the time to care for his fellow man.
And always keep on trying to give help where he can,
Then a better world would be made each day, so take a stand, lend a helping hand,
Then a better world would be made each day, together in spirit we are all as one.

Chorus Repeats

Musical Terms:

unis. (unison)   *mf* (mezzo forte)   *f* (forte)

Preparation:
Practice this rhythm pattern before you sing the song.

Now look at measure 25. What do you notice about the rhythm there? How many times does that pattern appear in this song? Reading a new song is much easier when you notice repeated patterns.

Evaluation:
An important part of being a performer is the ability to express your feelings to an audience. After you have learned "We Belong," videotape your choir singing this song. Does your face express what the song means to you? Write an essay discussing what the words of "We Belong" mean to you.

To my friend and inspiration, John Jacobson

We Belong

For SATB and Piano

Words and Music by LINDA SPEVACEK

nit-ed we stand,__ strong in spir-it we are all as

nit-ed we stand,__ strong in spir-it we are all as

C   G/B   AMI   EMI/B C6   C   CMA7/D C6/D Dsus7 D7

one._____   If

one._____

C/G G   AMI/D G   C/G G   AMI/D G

Alto *mf*

ev-'ry-one__ would take the time__ to care for his fel-low man.__

G   D/G   C/G   D/G

mf

165

168

long,_____ here we stand_ u - nit-ed we stand,_

long,_____ here we stand_ u - nit-ed we stand,_

C/E EMI⁷ G/D   C   G/B   C   G/B   C   G/B

strong in spir - it we are

strong in spir - it we are

AMI   G/B   C⁶   C   Dsus   D

103

one!_____

one!_____

one!_____

103 C/G G   C/G G   C/G G   Gadd 9

ff   gva   loco

171

GLOSSARY

a cappella [It.] (ah-kah-PEH-lah) - Singing without instrumental accompaniment.

accelerando (*accel.*) [It.] (ahk-chel-leh-RAHN-doh) - Becoming faster; a gradual increase in tempo.

accent (>) - Stress or emphasize a note (or chord) over others around it. Accents occur by singing the note louder or stressing the beginning consonant or vowel.

accidentals - Symbols that move the pitch up or down a half step.

- sharp (♯) - raises the pitch one half step.
- flat (♭) - lowers the pitch one half step.
- natural (♮) - cancels a previous *sharp* or *flat*. (When it cancels a flat, the pitch is raised one half step; when it cancels a sharp, the pitch is lowered one half step).

Accidentals affect all notes of the same pitch that follow the accidental within the same measure, or if an altered note is *tied* over a *barline*.

adagio [It.] (ah-DAH-jee-oh) - Tempo marking indicating slow.

al fine [It.] (ahl FEE-neh) - To ending. An indicator following *D.C.* or *D.S.* From the Latin *finis,* "to finish."

allargando (*allarg.*) [It.] (ahl-lar-GAHN-doh) - Broadening, becoming slower, sometimes with an accompanying *crescendo.*

allegro [It.] (ah-LEH-groh) - Tempo marking indicating fast.

alto - A treble voice that is lower than the *soprano,* usually written in the *treble clef.*

andante [It.] (ahn-DAHN-teh) - Tempo marking indicating medium or "walking" tempo.

animato [It.] (ah-nee-MAH-toh) - Style marking meaning animated.

arranger - The person who takes an already existing composition and reorganizes it to fit a new instrumentation or voicing.

articulation - The clear pronunciation of text using the lips, teeth, and tongue. The singer must attack consonants crisply and use proper vowel formation.

a tempo - Return to the original tempo.

balletto [It.] (bah-LEH-toh) - A 16th century vocal composition with dance-rhythms and often phrases of nonsense syllables like "fa-la-la." Giovanni Gastoldi wrote the earliest known collection of balletti.

bar - See *measure.*

barline - A vertical line that divides the staff into smaller sections called measures. A double barline indicates the end of a section or piece of music.

| Barline | Double Barline |

Baroque Period (ca. 1600-1750) - (bah-ROHK) The period in Western music history that extended from 1600 to about 1750; also the musical styles of that period. The style features of most Baroque music are frequent use of *polyphony*; fast, motor-like rhythms; and use of the chorale. Some famous Baroque composers were J.S. Bach, G.F. Handel, and Antonio Vivaldi.

bass - A male voice written in *bass clef* that is lower than a *tenor* voice.

bass clef - The symbol at the beginning of the staff used for lower voices and instruments, and the piano left hand. It generally refers to pitches lower than *middle C*. The two dots are on either side of F, so it is often referred to as the F clef.

beat - The unit of recurring pulse in music.

breath mark (,) - An indicator within a phrase or melody where the musician should breathe. See also *no breath* and *phrase marking*.

caesura (//) [Fr.] (seh-SHOO-rah) - A break or pause between two musical phrases. Also called a *break*.

call and response - Alternation between two performers or groups of performers. Often used in *spirituals*, this technique begins with a leader (or group) singing a phrase followed by a response of the same phrase (or continuation of the phrase) by a second group.

canon - A musical form in which a melody in one part is followed a short time later by other parts performing the same melody. Canons are sometimes called *rounds*.

cantata [It.] (cahn-TAH-tah) - A large work (originally sacred) involving solos, chorus, organ, and occasionally orchestra. The cantata tells a story through text and music. Johann Sebastian Bach wrote a cantata for each Sunday of the church year.

chantey - A song sung by sailors in rhythm with their work.

chord - Three or more pitches sounding at the same time or in succession as in a broken chord. See also *interval*.

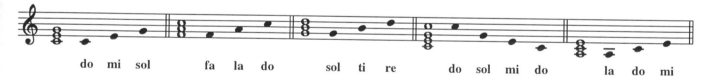

chromatic - Moving up or down by half steps, often outside of the key. Also the name of a scale composed entirely of half steps (all twelve pitches within an *octave*). The chromatic scale is distinct from the *diatonic* scale.

Classical Period (ca. 1750-1835) - The period in Western music history began in Italy in 1750 and continued until about 1825. Music of the Classical Period emphasized balance of phrase and structure. Ludwig von Beethoven, W.A. Mozart, and Joseph Haydn were famous composers from the Classical Period.

clef - The symbol at the beginning of the staff that identifies a set of pitches. See also *bass clef* and *treble clef*.

coda (⊕) [It.] (COH-dah) - Ending. A concluding portion of a composition.

common time (C) - Another name for the meter 4/4. See also *cut time*.

composer - The writer or creator of a song or musical composition. See also *arranger*.

compound meter - Meters which have a multiple of 3 such as 6 or 9 (but not 3 itself). Compound meter reflects the note that receives the division unlike *simple meter*. (Ex. 6/8 = six divisions to the beat in two groups of three where the eighth note receives one division). An exception to the compound meter rule is when the music occurs at a slow tempo, then the music is felt in beats rather than divisions. See also *meter* and *time signature*.

con [It.] (kawn) - With.

crescendo (*cresc.* or ⟨) [It.] (kreh-SHEN-doh) - Gradually growing louder. The opposite of *decrescendo*.

cued notes - Smaller notes indicating either *optional harmony* or notes from another voice part.

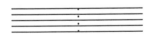

cut time (¢) - 2/2 time, the half note gets the beat.

da capo (D.C.) [It.] (dah KAH-poh) - Repeat from the beginning. See also *dal segno* and *al fine*.

dal segno (D.S.) [It.] (dahl SAYN-yoh) - Go back to the sign (𝄋) and repeat.

D.C. al fine [It.] - Repeat from the beginning to *fine* or end. See also *da capo* and *al fine*.

decrescendo (*decresc.* or ⟩) [It.] (deh-kreh-SHEN-doh) - Gradually growing softer. The opposite of *crescendo*. See also *diminuendo*.

descant - A high ornamental voice part often lying above the melody.

diatonic - Step by step movement within a regular scale (any key). A combination of the seven whole and half steps (of different pitch names) in a key. Distinct from *chromatic*.

diminuendo (*dim.*) [It.] (dih-min-new-EN-doh) - Gradually growing softer. See also *decrescendo*.

diphthong (DIPH-thong) - A combination of two vowel sounds consisting of a primary vowel sound and a secondary vowel sound. The secondary vowel sound is (usually) at the very end of the diphthong. (Ex. The word "I" is really a diphthong using an "ah" and an "ee." The "ee" is a very brief sound at the end of the word.)

divisi (div.) [It.] (dee-VEE-see) - Divide; the parts divide.

dolce [It.] (DOHL-cheh) - Sweetly; usually soft as well.

dotted barline - A "helper" *barline* in songs with unusual *time signatures* such as 5/8 and 7/8. The dotted barline helps divide the measure into two or more divisions of *triple* or *duple* beat groups.

downbeat - The accented first beat of the measure.

D.S. al Coda [It.] (ahl KOH-dah) - Repeat from the sign (𝄋) and sing the *coda* when you see the symbol (𝄌).

D.S. al fine [It.] (ahl FEE-neh) - Repeat from the sign (𝄋) to *fine* or ending.

duple - Any *time signature* or group of beats that is a multiple of 2.

dynamic - The loudness or softness of a line of music. Dynamic changes may occur frequently within a composition.

endings - ⌐1.   ⌐2.   (First and second endings) Alternate endings to a repeated section.

enharmonic - Identical tones which are named and written differently. For instance, F-sharp and G-flat are the same note, they are "enharmonic" with each other.

ensemble - A group of musicians, (instrumentalists, singers, or some combination) who perform together.

fermata (⌢) [It.] (fur-MAH-tah) - Hold the indicated note (or rest) for longer than its value; the length is left up to the interpretation of the director or the performer.

fine [It.] (FEE-neh) - Ending. From the Latin *finis*, "to finish."

flat (♭) -An *accidental* that lowers the pitch of a note one half step. Flat also refers to faulty intonation when the notes are sung or played sightly under the correct pitch.

forte (*f*) [It.] (FOR-teh) - Loud.

fortissimo (*ff*) [It.] (for-TEE-see-moh) - Very loud.

freely - A style marking permitting liberties with tempo, dynamics, and style. *Rubato* may also be incorporated.

grand staff - A grouping of two staves.

half step - The smallest distance (or *interval*) between two notes on a keyboard. Shown symbolically (v). The *chromatic* scale is composed entirely of half steps.

half time - See *cut time*.

harmonic interval - *Intervals* played simultaneously.

harmony - Two or more musical tones sounding simultaneously.

hemiola [Gr.] (hee-mee-OH-lah) - A unique rhythmical device in which the beat of a *triple meter* has the feeling of d*uple meter* (or the reverse) regardless of *barlines* and *time signatures*. This is accomplished through *ties* and/or *accent* placement.

homophony [Gr.] (haw-MAW-faw-nee) - Music in which melodic interest is concentrated in one voice part and may have subordinate accompaniment (distinct from *polyphony* in which all voice parts are equal). Homophony is also music which consists of two or more voice parts with similar or identical rhythms. From the Greek words meaning "same sounds," homophony could be described as being "hymn-style."

hushed - A style marking indicating a soft, whispered tone.

interval - The distance between two pitches.

intonation - Accuracy of pitch.

key - The organization of tonality around a single pitch (*key-note*). See also *key-note* and *key signature*.

key-note - The pitch which is the tonal center of a key. The first tone (note) of a scale. It is also called the *tonic*. A key is named after the key-note; for example in the key of A-flat, A-flat is the key-note. See also *key* and *key signature*.

key signature - The group of *sharps* or *flats* at the beginning of a staff which combine to indicate the locations of the key-note and configuration of the *scale*. If there are no sharps or flats, the key is automatically C major or A minor.

 B♭ major or G minor

legato [It.] (leh-GAH-toh) - Smooth and connected. Opposite of *staccato*.

ledger lines (or leger lines) - The short lines used to extend the lines and spaces of the *staff*.

leggiero [It.] (leh-JEE-roh) - Light articulation; sometimes non-*legato*.

macaronic text - Text in which two languages are used (usually Latin and one other language).

madrigal - A kind of 16th century Italian composition based on secular poetry. Madrigals were popular into the 17th century.

maestoso [It.] (mah-ee-STOH-soh) - Majestic.

major key/scale/mode - A specific arrangement of whole steps and half steps in the following order:

Letter Names:	G	A	B	C	D	E	F♯	G
Moveable Do:	do	re	mi	fa	sol	la	ti	do
Fixed Do:	sol	la	ti	do	re	mi	fi	sol
Numbers:	1	2	3	4	5	6	7	1

See also *minor key/scale/mode*.

marcato [It.] (mahr-KAH-toh) - Marked or stressed, march-like.

mass - The central religious service of the Roman Catholic Church. It consists of several sections divided into two groups: Proper of the Mass (text changes for every day) and Ordinary of the Mass (text stays the same in every mass). Between the years 1400 and 1600 the mass assumed its present form consisting of the Kyrie, Gloria, Credo, Sanctus, and Agnus Dei. It may include chants, hymns, and psalms as well. The mass also developed into large musical works for chorus, soloists, and even orchestra.

measure - A group of beats divided by *barlines*. Measures are sometimes called *bars*. The first beat of each measure is usually accented.

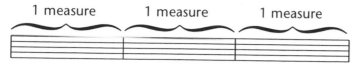

melisma - Long groups of notes sung on one syllable of text.

melodic interval - Notes that comprise an *interval* played in succession.

melody - A succession of musical tones; also the predominant line in a song.

meter - A form of rhythmic organization (grouping of beats). The kind of meter designated by the *time signature*. See also *simple* and *compound meters*.

meter signature - See *time signature*.

metronome marking - A marking which appears over the top staff of music which indicates the kind of note which will get the beat, and the number of beats per minute as measured by a metronome. It reveals the *tempo*. (Ex. (♩ = 100)).

mezzo forte (*mf*) [It.] (MEH-tsoh FOR-teh) - Medium loud.

mezzo piano (*mp*) [It.] (MEH-tsoh pee-AH-noh) - Medium soft.

middle C - The C which is located closest to the middle of the piano keyboard. Middle C can be written in either the *treble* or *bass clef*.

minor key/scale/mode - A specific arrangement of whole steps and half steps in the following order:

Letter Names:	D	E	F	G	A	B♭	C	D
Moveable La:	la	ti	do	re	mi	fa	sol	la
Fixed La:	re	mi	fa	sol	la	te	do	re
Numbers:	1	2	3	4	5	6	7	1

See also *major key/scale/mode.*

mixed meter - Frequently changing meters or *time signatures* within a piece of music.

modulation - Changing keys within a song. Adjust to the *key signature*, the *key-note*, and proceed.

molto [It.] (MOHL-toh) - Much, very. (Ex. molto rit. = greatly slowing).

monophony - Music which consists of a single melody. This earliest form of composition is from the Greek words meaning "one sound." Chant or plainsong is monophony.

mosso [It.] (MOH-soh) - Moved, agitated.

mysterioso [It.] (mih-steer-ee-OH-soh) - A style marking indicating a mysterious or haunting mood.

natural (♮) - Cancels a previous *sharp* (♯) or *flat* (♭). (When it cancels a flat, the pitch is raised one half step; when it cancels a sharp, the pitch is lowered one half step.)

no breath (♩ ♩ or N.B.) - An indication by either the *composer/arranger* or the editor of where *not* to breathe in a line of music. See also *phrase marking*.

notation - All written notes and symbols which are used to represent music.

octave - The *interval* between two notes of the same name. Octaves can be indicated within a score using 8va (octave above) and 8vb (octave below).

1 octave

C   C
do   do

ostinato [It.] (ah-stee-NAH-toh) - A repeated pattern used as a harmonic basis.

optional divisi (opt. div.) [It.] (dee-VEE-see) - The part splits into optional harmony. The smaller sized *cued notes* indicate the optional notes to be used.

phrase marking (⌒) - An indication by either the *composer* or the *arranger* as to the length of a line of music or melody. This marking often means that the musician is not to breathe during its duration. See also *no breath*.

piano (*p*) [It.] (pee-AH-noh) - Soft.

pianissimo (*pp*) [It.] (pee-ah-NEE-see-moh) - Very soft.

pick-up - An incomplete measure at the beginning of a song or phrase.

pitch - The highness or lowness of musical sounds.

più [It.] (pew) - More. (Ex. più forte or più mosso allegro).

poco [It.] (POH-koh) - Little. (Ex. poco cresc. = a little crescendo).

poco a poco [It.] (POH-koh ah POH-koh) - Little by little (Ex. poco a poco cresc. = increase in volume, little by little).

polyphony [Gr.] (pahw-LIH-fahw-nee) - Music which consist of two or more independent melodies which combine to create simultaneous voice parts with different rhythms. Polyphony often involves contrasting dynamics and imitation from part to part. From the Greek words meaning "many sounds," polyphony is sometimes called counterpoint.

presto [It.] (PREH-stoh) - Very fast.

rallentando (*rall.*) [It.] (rahl-en-TAHN-doh) - Gradually slower. See also *ritardando*.

relative major/minor - Major and minor tonalities which share the same *key signature*.

G major   E minor

Renaissance Period (ca. 1450-1600) (REHN-neh-sahns) - A period in the Western world following the Middle Ages. Renaissance means "rebirth" and was a celebration of entrance into the modern age of thought and invention. In music it was a period of great advancement in notation and compositional ideas. *Polyphony* was developing and the *madrigal* became popular. Orlando di Lasso, Giovanni da Palestrina, Tomás Luis de Victoria, and Josquin Des Prez were some of the more famous Renaissance composers.

repeat sign (‖: :‖) - Repeat the section. If the repeat sign is omitted, go back to the beginning. See also *endings*.

resolution (res.) - A progression from a dissonant tone or harmony to a consonant harmony. (Usually approached by step.) See also *suspension*.

rhythm - The organization of non-pitched sounds in time. Rhythm encompasses note and rest duration as well as *meters*, *tempos*, and their relationships.

ritardando (*rit.*) [It.] (ree-tahr-DAHN-doh) - Gradually slower. See also *rallentando*.

Romantic Period (ca. 1825-1900) - A period in 19th century Western art, literature, and music that lasted into the early 20th century. In music, as well as the other areas, Romanticism focused on the emotion of art. Works from this period emphasized the emotional effect music has on the listener through dynamic contrasts and different ways of changing the "mood." Opera flourished as well as chamber music. Some famous Romantic composers are Franz Schubert, Frederick Chopin, Hector Berlioz, Johannes Brahms, and Richard Wagner.

root tone - The lowest note of a *triad* in its original position; the note on which the chord is built and named.

round - see *canon*.

rubato [It.] (roo-BAH-toh) - The tempo is free, left up to the interpretation of the director or performer.

scale - An inventory or collection of pitches. The word "scale" (from the Italian *scala*) means ladder. Thus, many musical scales are a succession of pitches higher and lower.

do re mi fa sol la ti do
G major

la ti do re mi fa sol la
E minor

score - The arrangement of a group of vocal and instrumental staffs which all sound at the same time.

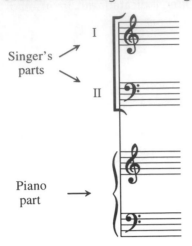

sempre [It.] (SEHM-preh) - Always , continually. (Ex. sempre forte = always loud)

sequence - The successive repetition of a short melodic idea at different pitch levels.

sequence

sharp (♯) - An *accidental* that raises the pitch of a note one half step. Also, faulty intonation in which the note is sung slightly above the correct pitch.

sign (𝄋 **or Segno**) [It.] (SAYN-yoh) - A symbol that marks the place in music where the musician is to skip back to from the *dal Segno* (*D.S.*).

simile (*sim.*) [It.] - (SIM-eh-lee) Continue the same way.

simple meter - Meters which are based upon the note which receives the beat. (Ex. 4/4 or 𝄵 is based upon the quarter note receiving the beat.)

skip - The melodic movement of one note to another in *intervals* larger than a step.

slide (⟋♩) - To approach a note from underneath the designated pitch and "slide" up to the correct pitch. Slides often appear in jazz, pop tunes, and *spirituals*.

slur (⌢) - A curved line placed above or below a group of notes to indicate that they are to be sung on the same text syllable. Slurs are also used in instrumental music to indicate that the group of notes should be performed *legato* (smoothly connected).

solfège [Fr.] (SOHL-fehj) - The study of sight-singing using pitch syllables (do re mi, etc.).

soprano - The highest treble voice, usually written in *treble clef.*

spirito [It.] (SPEE-ree-toh) - Spirit.

spiritual - Religious folk songs of African American origin associated with work, recreation, or religious gatherings. They developed prior to the Civil War and are still influential today. They have a strong rhythmic character and are often structured in *call and response.*

spoken - Reciting text with the speaking voice rather than singing the designated line. Often indicated with 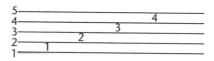 instead of notes.

staccato ( ) [It.] (stah-KAH-toh -) Short, separated notes. Opposite of *legato*.

staff - The five horizontal parallel lines and four spaces between them on which notes are placed to show *pitch*.

The lines and spaces are numbered from the bottom up.

step - Melodic movement from one note to the next higher or lower *scale* degree.

style marking - An indicator at the beginning of a song or section of song which tells the musician in general what style the music should be performed. (Ex. *freely* or *animato*)

subito (*sub.*) [It.] (SOO-bee-toh) - Suddenly. (Ex. sub. piano = suddenly soft)

suspension (sus.) - The sustaining or "suspending" of a pitch from a consonant chord into a dissonant chord often using a *tie*. The resulting dissonant chord then *resolves* to a consonant chord. The musical effect is one of tension and release. See also *resolution*.

swing - A change in interpretation of eighth note durations in some music (often jazz and blues). Groups of two eighth notes ( ) are no longer sung evenly, instead they are performed like part of a *triplet* ( ). The eighth notes still appear . A swing style is usually indicated at the beginning of a song or section. (=).

syllables - Names given to pitch units or rhythm units to aid in sight-reading.

do re mi

ta	ta	ti	ti	ta
1	2	3	&	4

syncopation - The use of *accents* and *ties* to create rhythmic interest. The result is a rhythmic pattern which stresses notes on the off beat. This technique is commonly found in *spirituals and jazz*.

tempo - The speed of the beat.

tempo primo [It.] (TEHM-poh PREE-moh) - Return to the first (*primo*) tempo. See *Tempo I*.

tempo I - Return to the first tempo. Also called tempo primo.

tenor - A male voice written in *bass clef* or *treble clef*. It is lower than the *alto*, but higher than the *bass*.

tenuto ( ) [It.] (teh-NOO-toh) - A slight stress on the indicated note. The note is held for its full value.

texture - The interrelationship of the voices and/or instruments within a piece of music. *Monophonic, homophonic,* and *polyphonic* are all types of textures.

181

tie ( ) - A line connecting two or more notes of the same pitch so that their durations are their combined sum. Often occurring over *barlines*.

time signature - The symbol placed at the beginning of a composition or section to indicate its meter. This most often takes the form of a fraction (⁴⁄4 or ³⁄4), but may also involve a symbol as in the case of common time (c) and cut time (¢). The upper number indicates the number of beats in a measure and the lower number indicates which type of note receiving the beat. (An exception occurs in *compound meters*. See *compound meter* for an explanation.)

to coda - Go to the ⊕ .

tonality - The organization of *pitches* in a song in which a certain pitch (tone) is designated as the *key-note* or the note which is the tonal center of a *key*.

tone - A musical sound of definite pitch and quality.

tonic - The *key-note* of a key or scale.

tonic chord - The name given to the chord built on the *key-note* of the scale.

transpose - To rewrite or perform a song in a *key* other than the original.

treble clef - The symbol at the beginning of the staff used for higher voices and instruments, and the piano right hand. It generally refers to pitches higher then *middle* C. The curve is wrapped around the G, as a result it is also called the G clef.

triad - A special type of 3-note chord built in 3rds over a *root tone*.

trill (*tr* ∿∿∿) - Rapid alteration (within a key) between the marked note and the one above it.

triple - Any *time signature* or group of beats that is a multiple of 3.

triplet - A borrowed division of the beat where three notes of equal duration are to be sung in the time normally occupied by two notes of equal duration. Usually indicated with a 3.

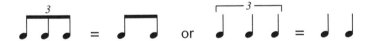

unison (unis.) - All parts singing the same notes at the same time, (or singing in *octaves*).

villancico [Sp.] (vee-yahn-SEE-koh or bee-yahn-SEE-koh) - A composition of Spanish origin from the 15th and 16th centuries. Similar to the *madrigal*, this type of work is based on secular poetry and is structured around the verses and refrains of its text.

vivace [It.] (vee-VAH-cheh) - Very fast.

whole step - The combination of two successive half steps. Shown symbolically (⊔).

# TO THE TEACHER

Why We Wrote This Book

We created this series because we are vitally committed to the nurturing of choral music, to the more effective teaching of choral music, and particularly to the encouragement of the young musicians who perform choral music. We believe that every child is musically expressive and deserves the opportunity to explore that capacity.

Too often, our definitions of literacy have been limited to words on paper. Although aspects of music can be taught as the written word (i.e., as a series of facts or as a written symbolic language), ultimately music is perhaps not best understood through the written word, but rather as a unique way of looking at the world, a special dimension of human understanding. What one understands, expresses, or feels when performing choral music is indeed "another way of knowing." We believe that it is vital that our children be given opportunities to experience this expanded literacy.

Janice Killian   **Michael O'Hern**   **Linda Rann**

About the Series

The four levels of *Essential Repertoire* (Young Choir, Developing Choir, Concert Choir, and Concert Choir - Artist Level) contain choral literature especially selected for choirs of differing ages and experience levels.

Level I, *Essential Repertoire for the Young Choir*, contains selections which take into account the limitations of the early adolescent voice. It contains musically accessible pieces which would be ideal for the beginning of the year, as well as selections appropriate for later in the year, or for groups which are ready for a special challenge. *Essential Repertoire for the Young Choir* is specifically designed for seventh and eighth graders, but the material included might be appropriate for any chorus, regardless of age.

Features of the Program

Each repertoire book contains a wide range of literature:

- a variety of historical periods
- a variety of other countries and cultures
- a mixture of English and foreign-language texts
- a variety of challenging and beginning level songs
- a mixture of styles: masterworks, folksongs and spirituals; a cappella and accompanied pieces; sacred and secular works; arrangements of familiar songs; and a few pop-style selections

Every effort was made to select high quality, time-tested literature.

Each song is independent of the others, i.e. there is no special sequence intended. Little prior knowledge is assumed on the part of the student. Teachers are encouraged to make selections as needed to create a varied and meaningful classroom and concert program.

Student information pages are included with each choral selection to help students learn basic musical skills, to be introduced to the cultural context in which the music was created and to evaluate their own progress.

The Teacher Editions contain the same information as the student text, plus much additional background information, as well as suggested lesson plans, vocal warm-ups, and performance tips.

The repertoire books are designed to be used in conjunction with *Essential Musicianship*, Book 1, a comprehensive choral method for teaching vocal technique, sight-singing, and music theory.

How to Use *Essential Repertoire for the Young Choir*

Each song is treated as an independent unit of study. Prior to each song is a page of information designed to be read by the student. Student pages consist of:

- Title and Composer, text information, and voicing/instrumentation
- Cultural context of the song: Usually students can read and understand this section with limited guidance from the teacher.
- Musical terms: Students should be encouraged to find the listed terms in the song, and look up any unknown terms and/or symbols in the glossary.
- Preparation: Students will usually need teacher assistance in completing the Preparation section. This book is not designed to be student self-paced. Additional teaching suggestions, background information and performance tips are included in the Teacher Edition.
- Evaluation: In most cases the Evaluation section is to be completed after the notes and rhythms of the piece have been mastered. Details for guiding the students' evaluation appear in the Teacher Edition.

Students should be encouraged to read the Cultural Context and Musical Terms sections of of the text page prior to learning the song. This could be an effective activity for students while the teacher is involved in taking roll or other tasks. Students will usually need assistance in completing the rest of the text page.

The Teacher Edition

The Teacher Edition includes an extensive lesson plan for each choral selection which may be taught as suggested, expanded over a six-week period, or modified as needed. Each teaching plan contains the following:

- Student Text Page (slightly reduced in size)
- Ranges and song information (key, meter, form, performance possibilities)
- Learning objectives (Essential Elements) for each song correlated with the National Standards for Arts Education
- Historical/stylistic guidelines
- Answers to any student page questions
- Vocal technique/warm-ups/exercises
- Rehearsal guidelines and notes: 1) Suggested teaching sequence, and 2) Performance tips
- Evaluation suggestions for assessing student progress on the stated objectives
- Extension ideas

Who Should Use This Book

The authors of this text, all currently-practicing choral educators, bring a combined total of more than fifty years experience to the writing of this text. Their careful suggestions of tried and proven techniques provide a valuable resource of choral ideas for polishing performances.

Choral directors who are just entering the profession are encouraged to follow the suggested teaching sequence as written for each song to gain practical teaching skills.

Experienced choral directors may want to refer to the performance tips as a source of ideas for approaching a piece and refining it.

The warmups, vocalises, or polishing exercises included for every song in the Teacher Edition may be particularly applicable to a given song. They contain a wealth of ideas and suggestions which may be applied to other choral situations.

In Conclusion

Essential Repertoire for the Young Choir, when combined with the companion volume *Essential Musicianship*, is in essence, a complete curriculum for the choral experience — a core library of repertoire aimed at awakening the singer's potential for self development, musical expression, and personal esteem.

JANICE KILLIAN received degrees from the University of Kansas, University of Connecticut, and earned her Ph.D. from the University of Texas-Austin. Throughout her career she has focused primarily on the junior high choral experience, but her teaching background includes K-12 public school experiences in Kansas, Connecticut, Minnesota, and Texas, as well as higher education experience at the State University of New York at Buffalo. Currently Dr. Killian is a member of the music faculty at Texas Woman's University in Denton, Texas, where her duties include directing a choral ensemble, teaching graduate and undergraduate music education classes, and conducting music education research.

MICHAEL O'HERN has been the choral director at Lake Highlands Junior High in Richardson, Texas, since the fall of 1982. A graduate of West Texas State University, Mr. O'Hern has completed graduate work at East Texas State University and The University of Texas at Arlington. A former RISE Foundation "Teacher of the Year" for the Richardson School District, Mr. O'Hern is often called upon to serve as a clinician and adjudicator throughout Texas. He serves as a soloist throughout the Dallas area. His choirs have won numerous awards at local, state, and national competitions. The Lake Highlands Junior High Chorale performed for the Texas Music Educators Convention in 1989 and 1994.

LINDA RANN has earned undergraduate and graduate degrees in Music Education from Louisiana State University in Baton Rouge with additional studies at Sam Houston State University, Texas Woman's University, University of North Texas, and Westminster Choir College. She is currently choral director at Dan Long Middle School in the Carrollton-Farmers Branch I.S.D., Carrollton, Texas, where her choirs are consistent sweepstakes winners. With over twenty years of public school teaching experience in elementary and middle school vocal music, Mrs. Rann is a frequent choral clinician and adjudicator. She has presented workshops nationally in the areas of middle school choral music and assessment in the performing arts.